A MOMENT TO BREATHE

A MOMENT TO BREATHE

Sermonic Reflections

Rev. Amenti Sujai, PhD
Rev. Daniel T. Hembree, PhD

Advocate Press, Columbia, South Carolina

Copyright © 2025 by Advocate Press

All rights reserved. No part of this book may be reproduced or transmitted in any form or by any means, electronic or mechanical, including photocopying, recording, or by any information storage and retrieval system, without permission in writing from the publisher.

First published in the United States of America in 2025

Library of Congress Cataloging-in-Publication Data
A Moment to Breathe
p. cm.

ISBN 978-1-966237-09-9

For you who serve out of love.

Your breath is your anchor
every inhale is a new experience,
every exhale is an opportunity to let go.

Table of Contents

Introduction ix
Patience 1
Peace 5
Know Who You Are 9
Love Yourself 13
Challenges 17
Be Joyful 21
Divine Possibilities 25
Plan Your Next Victory 29
When You Feel Invisible 33
Breathe 37
Choices 41
Don't Be Afraid to Fail 45
Blessings 49
What Is Required? 53
Something New 57
Get in the Race 61
Another Perspective 65
A Radical Kind of Love 69
Beginnings 73
Passing the Peace 77
Do Not Forget to Remember 81
About the Authors 85

Introduction

Welcome to a journey of spiritual growth and introspection. This book explores the profound messages of patience, peace, identity, self-love, challenges, joy, divine possibilities, victory, visibility, breathing, choices, failure, blessings, duty, and renewal as depicted in the scriptures. Drawing from biblical narratives and personal reflections, this text offers guidance, comfort, and wisdom for those navigating the complexities of life and faith.

Our exploration begins with a deep dive into the concept of patience, illustrated through the teachings of James and the historical endurance of our spiritual ancestors. We consider the virtues of peace and reflection while encouraging a disconnect from the outer noise to find tranquility within. The stories of biblical figures like Daniel and David teach us about identity and the importance of knowing oneself in the face of adversity.

Love, both of self and others, is examined through James's teachings, which urge us to balance compassion toward others with care for ourselves. We confront challenges through Matthew's lens, learning how to transform our trials into triumphs with faith and community support. The joy of spiritual fulfillment is celebrated, inspired by David's ecstatic joy when embracing the Ark of the Covenant.

Through the narrative of John 14, we explore the limitless possibilities that faith in the divine opens up, urging readers to engage in acts of creation and service. The theme of victory encourages readers to plan and prevail through faith, drawing strength from the story of Joshua. We confront feelings of invisibility and insignificance by connecting deeply with the divine, ensuring we are seen, known, and valued beyond earthly recognition.

Breathing is redefined as a spiritual practice, reminding us of the divine breath that gives life and purpose. The divine breath is embedded in all of nature, and as we breathe, we breathe with all creation.

We ponder choices through Psalm 16, reflecting on the importance of choosing faith and courage over fear and complacency. The concept of failure is reimagined as a necessary step toward growth and ultimate success, inspired by the perseverance of Chadwick Boseman and biblical heroes.

Blessings are counted and cherished, and gratitude is called to be cultivated as a transformative practice that enhances spiritual and physical well-being. Finally, this work calls for a commitment to justice, mercy, and humility, as Micah encourages us to live lives that reflect these divine principles.

Each chapter invites you to pause, reflect, and engage with the teachings, incorporating them into your daily life to foster a deeper connection with the divine and a more fulfilled existence. This book is not just a collection of teachings; it is a companion in your spiritual journey, a source of continual inspiration and guidance as you navigate the path of faith, challenges, and discovery.

Pause. Breathe. Peace will find us in the space between every thought.

Chapter 1

Patience

James 5:7-10

We begin our journey of reflection drawing upon the wisdom of those who came before us. Our spiritual ancestors from various cultures and backgrounds demonstrate resilience, patience, and faith that echo through time. They encountered vast migrations and formidable adversities, always believing in a transformative future ordained by divine timing—a belief that supported their survival and propelled them toward freedom across centuries.

Consider the trials they faced, their aspirations, and their hopeful vigil for brighter days. Their endurance resonates with the teachings of James, who, in his epistle, guided an early Christian community through persecution and uncertainty. James redefined patience not as a passive waiting but as an active endurance. He urged his followers to live purposefully and with resolve, to continue striving for justice, peace, and love amid their trials while awaiting Christ's return.

The notion of patience often eludes us in moments of immediate suffering or injustice. James calls us to strengthen our hearts, an invitation to anchor ourselves in the expansive narrative of God's plan during trying times. This strength is not about ignoring our pain but facing it bravely, drawing inspiration from those who have endured.

Our ancestors, who weathered the storms of their tribulations, left us a legacy of perseverance and faith. Their lives illustrate that patience transcends mere waiting—it is about enduring gracefully, nurturing love, and fostering community under the weight of demanding challenges. We learn that even in the darkest times, we receive strength to continue our work, heal ourselves and our communities, and fully embrace our purpose. They instill the patience and faith necessary to believe in forthcoming change and embrace life's fullness.

As you face individuals or circumstances that challenge your patience today, remember the enduring spirit of our ancestors. Their experiences offer invaluable insight into perseverance and thriving. Engage deeply with every challenge, confront each with tenacity, and contribute positively to our community. Let their stories inspire you to embody compassion, understanding, and an unwavering commitment to the enduring values that have guided generations. With their spiritual legacy of faith, you have this gift of determination to act with patience, trusting that you are actively shaping the future just as our ancestors shaped theirs.

We do not passively wait for change but enact it with the wisdom and strength passed down to us.

The Meditation

Find a quiet spot to sit or lie down comfortably. Close your eyes, take a deep breath, and focus on being in the present. Notice the solidity of your body in the space, releasing any tightness or distractions. Inhale, hold it briefly, then breathe out slowly, letting go of stress or worries.

Imagine yourself as part of an unending narrative of history, marked by your ancestors' growing need to live their lives as they faced the unknown patiently. Perhaps your ancestors found themselves in places they had not wanted to be. Visualize the formidable strength and steadfast faith that helped them overcome obstacles and strive for freedom through many generations.

Inhale, drawing in the courage of your ancestors. As you exhale, let go of any impatience or despair, embracing the growth and development life demands. Patience involves more than waiting—it means living purposely and hopefully, even in tough times.

Think about James's teachings on a life dedicated to justice, peace, and love. See yourself as a part of this enduring quest, striving for a better world like those before you, driven by a spirit of optimism and resolve.

Now turn your attention inward. Reflect on your challenges or experiences of injustice. View these as chances to grow stronger when your patience is tested. Be inspired by the strength of those who previously endured much worse.

Continue deep breathing, contemplating the legacy of perseverance and faith left by your ancestors. They pressed on as they created, loved, and worked to build communities against incredible odds. Feel a connection to this legacy, discovering within yourself the joy, courage, and resolve to overcome sadness, discouragement, or fear.

With each breath in, invite joy and determination into your heart, equipping you to advance, speak your truth, heal, and live purposefully. With each breath out, release any doubts, fears, and uncertainties.

End your meditation with gratitude for your ancestors' gifts and lessons. Recognize your capacity for patience and faith, knowing you possess the strength to actively live your life as you await the changes you seek.

When you're ready, bring your awareness back to the present, feeling stable and revitalized. Open your eyes, prepared to carry on the legacy of patience.

The Questions

1. Considering your spiritual ancestors' historical resilience and faith, how can you incorporate their strength and patience into your life, particularly in times of personal challenge or uncertainty?

2. James's teachings emphasize patience as active endurance rather than passive waiting. How can this interpretation of patience influence how you approach your daily struggles or long-term goals, especially in contexts that demand justice, peace, and love?
3. The meditation invites you to connect deeply with the legacy of perseverance and faith left by those who came before us. What aspects of this legacy inspire you the most, and how can these qualities help you shape a more hopeful and purpose-driven future for yourself and your community?

Chapter 2

Peace

Philippians 4:4-8

In 2020, the candid words of a notable newspaper owner—who once declared, "News is something that somebody doesn't want to be printed; all the rest is advertising"—inspired me to embark on an experiment to live disconnected from the daily news. For two months, I (Amenti) withdrew from the relentless stream of information about COVID, politics, and the anger that hovered in the air. What unfolded was a remarkable transformation of my emotional and mental state—I felt less anxious and burdened by fear.

Reflecting on this period of media silence, it became evident that the narratives spun by experts and commentators were repetitive and stagnant, recycling the same ideas without offering tangible solutions or hope. Their words, lacking the power to instill peace or assurance, seemed to serve little more than the interests of their bosses and sponsors. This experience brought clarity: the omnipresent media, in all its forms, fundamentally aims to captivate our attention for profit, often at the expense of our peace.

The scriptures offer a poignant reflection on this phenomenon. In Paul's letter to the Philippians, specifically in the third chapter, he cautions the faithful against those who disrupt their serenity. The early Christians in Philippi faced external criticism from Jewish and non-Jewish communities, which could have easily sown discord and hindered their spiritual growth. Paul's guidance was clear: Ignore those who intend to disrupt and divide.

This historical backdrop mirrors our challenges in today's rapid, unending news environment. The world suggests many paths to peace—material wealth, political solutions, or even more conflict in the guise of eventual harmony. Yet these solutions fail to deliver true peace. They miss a fundamental truth: Peace is achieved through a daily commitment to withdraw from conflict and discord.

In Aramaic, the word for peace is *shalma*, which implies surrender. This surrender is not a sign of weakness but a voluntary act of goodwill toward others, an offer of tranquility without ulterior motives. Hebrew speakers would recognize this concept in the word *shalom*, which encompasses harmony and serenity. Thus, when we extend a greeting of peace, we commit to a relationship defined by mutual respect and calm.

However, embracing this kind of peace requires confronting our ego. The ego often mistrusts, fostering division rather than unity. Yet choosing to surrender in the name of peace challenges the ego's narrative that equates surrender with defeat. True peace, the peace of God, thrives on openness, trust, and the absence of hidden agendas.

We are called to cultivate this divine peace. It begins with small, daily acts: dismissing the ego, embracing trust, fostering understanding, and building relationships rooted in genuine concern for one another. It involves looking beyond the world's superficial promises to the deeper, enduring peace that only faith can provide.

So I ask you: What burdens your heart? Is it worry, mistrust, or perhaps the harsh judgments of others? Whatever it may be, scripture encourages us to lay these burdens down with gratitude and seek what truly nurtures our souls.

Today, as we continue navigating a world divided by disharmony and misinformation, we remember the strength of surrender and the power of a peaceful heart. As active participants in a divine symphony of peace, we orchestrate our lives in harmony with God's will, creating experiences founded on love and understanding.

The Meditation

Take a moment to find a quiet space, a sanctuary where you can sit undisturbed. Breathe deeply and let your shoulders drop away from the ears. Release any tension of the day. As you settle into this time of reflection, consider the power of stillness.

Imagine disconnecting from the daily news cycle, which often brings a barrage of information about political tensions, worldly anguish, and an air of discontent. Visualize yourself pushing away from the stream of relentless details, much like pushing a boat away from the chaotic shoreline into calmer waters.

As you breathe in peace and exhale tension, reflect on how the constant overwhelming amount of news may be shaping your thoughts and feelings. Notice any feelings of anxiety or fear diminishing as you distance yourself from these influences. Allow yourself to experience the tranquility that comes from this detachment.

Think about the words often repeated in the media—words that seem to recycle fear without offering hope or solutions. Acknowledge how these narratives, driven by the interests of others, may distract from deeper truths and inner peace.

In the stillness of your retreat, turn your thoughts to the wisdom found in Paul's letter to the Philippians. Remember his advice to the early Christians to disregard those who disturb their peace. Like them, you are invited to ignore the voices that seek to divide and unsettle.

Reflect on the concept of peace in the languages of scripture. In Aramaic, *shalma* signifies surrender, not as a defeat but as an offering of tranquility. Consider how you might embody these ideas in your daily interactions, extending peace and harmony to those around you.

As you meditate, confront the barriers to peace within yourself. Often, our thoughts foster mistrust and division. Contemplate the act of surrendering—mindfully choosing peace over conflict, unity over division. Embrace the peace of God, which thrives on openness and trust, free from hidden agendas.

Conclude your meditation by reflecting on the personal burdens you carry. Whether they are worries, mistrust, or the judgments of others, imagine laying them down at the feet of the divine, replacing them with gratitude. Seek what truly nurtures your soul.

As you return from this meditation, carry with you the strength found in surrender and the profound peace that comes from living in harmony with God's will. Let this peace guide your thoughts and actions as you navigate the complexities of life, always remembering the power of a peaceful heart.

The Questions

1. How might regularly consuming news influence your emotional and spiritual well-being? Consider how disconnecting, even temporarily, could alter your perspective or mood.
2. Reflect on shalma and shalom as forms of peace through surrender and harmony. How can you practically apply these principles in your daily interactions to cultivate a more peaceful community around you?
3. Consider the barriers to peace within yourself, such as ego or mistrust. What steps can you take to actively surrender these obstructions to God, fostering unity and peace in your relationships and community?

Chapter 3

Know Who You Are

Daniel 6:10-28

In the swirling currents of life's many challenges, the story of Daniel in the lion's den offers hope and strength. This narrative, extending through twenty-eight verses from ancient scripture, vividly illustrates enduring faith and divine intervention, which is especially relevant to us during difficult times.

Daniel, an East African Hebrew boy, found himself in captivity under the rule of King Nebuchadnezzar of Babylon. From an early age, Daniel and his friends demonstrated an unwavering commitment to their faith, choosing vegetables and water over the king's lavish meals as a fast, preparing themselves for service. This simple act of defiance illustrated their dedication to purity and wisdom, later elevating Daniel to high ranks within the kingdom.

Daniel grew into a position of influence, becoming one of the king's three vice presidents. His exceptional wisdom set him apart, stirring jealousy and resentment among his peers. This scenario is often the case in any setting where integrity and excellence set one apart. Like Daniel, we frequently face the scrutiny of those who would rather see us fail.

The plot against Daniel leads to the decree that no one should pray to any being other than King Darius. Daniel, whose name declares, "God is my judge," defies this order, leading to his placement in the lion's den. Here, we see the crux of his faith: Even in the face of certain death, Daniel remains committed to his God, showing us the power of faithfulness and the importance of knowing who we are in God's eyes.

Daniel's story powerfully reminds us of the role of identity and faith in spiritual leadership. Knowing who we are, who we serve, and to whom we ultimately answer can sustain us through our darkest times. Daniel's identity was so entwined with his faith that even the threat of death could not compel him to compromise. Further, the narrative teaches us God's protection. Daniel did not argue his way out of the den; he trusted.

There will be moments when human efforts falter, and one must rely solely on divine intervention. God's silencing the lions symbolizes God's power to quiet all forms of opposition and adversity.

Lastly, the story of Daniel in the lion's den is not just about individual endurance but also about communal faith. Daniel was not alone; his prayers and those of his ancestors fortified him. This communal aspect of prayer is vital for the spiritual path. The prayerful support system formed by those who came before us continues with us and provides a foundation that can withstand any trial.

As you reflect on Daniel's story, consider these three pivotal lessons: the importance of a defined and devout identity in God, the necessity of yielding to God's protection, and the strength found in the present and historical prayers of the faith community. These lessons underscore the challenges we face and the divine resources available. In the solitude of your reflection, as you meditate on Daniel's unwavering faith, let his story inspire you to embrace your identity in God, rely on God's protective power, and remember the collective strength of those who have walked the path of faith before you. Just as Daniel walked out of the lion's den unharmed, so, too, can you navigate your challenges, fortified by God's perfect love and enduring presence.

The Meditation

As you settle into a quiet space, allow your breath to deepen and your mind to open to the story of Daniel in the lion's den. This ancient narrative is not just a scriptural story but a beacon for spiritual leaders, echoing through time with its lessons of faith and integrity.

Imagine Daniel, a young boy from the Hebrew lands who was now a captive in Babylon. From a young age, he and his friends chose a simple path—opting for vegetables and water over lavish royal feasts. This choice was their first step toward spiritual depth, laying a foundation of wisdom and humility to elevate Daniel to high places.

Breathe in and envision Daniel's rise to become one of the king's most trusted advisors, noted for his honesty and sharp perception. Exhale any feelings of envy or spite you perceive around you, recognizing, as Daniel did, that virtues often inspire both admiration and jealousy.

Inhale as you contemplate the decree that forbade prayers to anyone but King Darius. Daniel, steadfast in his faith, chose divine obedience over personal safety. During your exhale, picture him in the lion's den, surrounded yet untouched, his faith a shield of calm amid potential danger.

This meditation brings forth three insights for your spiritual path: the importance of a clear identity anchored in your faith, the peace derived from unwavering trust in divine protection, and the comfort of belonging to a community of believers.

As you breathe deeply, let Daniel's courage inspire you to affirm your spiritual identity. Trust in the protective embrace of your faith as you face your challenges. Remember, like Daniel, you are supported by many prayers and a divine presence continually by your side.

May this meditation renew and strengthen you, guiding you safely through your trials, just as Daniel emerged unscathed—empowered and affirmed by the boundless love and enduring care of the divine.

The Questions

1. Reflect on when you felt pressured to compromise your values.

How did you respond, and what did you learn about yourself from that experience?
2. Consider the concept of divine protection in your own life. How do you perceive and experience divine guidance and safeguarding during challenging times?
3. Think about the role of community in your spiritual journey. How has being part of a faith community influenced your growth and resilience in facing life's trials?

Chapter 4

Love Yourself

James 2:1-8

We often shoulder the spiritual, emotional, and sometimes physical needs of work, family, and other responsibilities. We immerse ourselves in the life of Jesus, strive to embody his teachings, and lead our communities through valleys and peaks. Yet in our sincere dedication to serving others, we might overlook the necessity of nurturing our spirits. This reflection on James's letter reminds us of the integral balance between loving others and ourselves.

Imagine the early Christian communities that James addressed. They faced dire risks for their faith—persecution was not a distant threat but a present danger. In such tumultuous times, the allure to prioritize the wealthy, who could offer protection or influence, must have been strong. Yet James saw this as a deviation from the core teachings of Christ. His warning was clear: True faith in Jesus is demonstrated through actions that uphold justice and equality, especially for the marginalized and oppressed. His critique wasn't just about societal ethics; it was a profound spiritual urging to realign with the principles of their faith.

The principle of loving your neighbor as yourself isn't solely about external actions; it's equally about internal harmony and recognition of our worth. Often, we find it easier to extend compassion outward than inward. But the royal law of love calls for a balance—it asks us to see ourselves through God's eyes as beings worthy of love, respect, and care.

Consider the impact of self-love in ministry. When we genuinely appreciate and value ourselves, we model a healthy spiritual life to our congregations. We teach by example that everyone reflects the divine and deserves love and care. This self-appreciation isn't vanity. It is an acknowledgment of our intrinsic worth that empowers us to serve others more effectively and with a joyous heart.

Furthermore, self-love equips us to navigate the challenges of ministry without burning out. It allows us to set boundaries, prioritize our well-being, and find peace even when external circumstances are chaotic. By loving ourselves, we maintain our resilience, ensuring that we can continue to be a source of strength for others.

Embracing love means forming a deeper connection with our congregations, and addressing our needs enables us to attune to the needs of others. This mutual understanding fosters a stronger, more compassionate community united in faith and love.

Remember that loving yourself is not a diversion from your spiritual duties but a fundamental part of fulfilling them. It is what sustains your ability to love others fervently and without reserve. You also honor the Creator who made you, loves you, and desires your wholeness.

Take heart in the knowledge that every step toward self-love is a step toward a more authentic ministry. Love yourself boldly and unapologetically, for it is in loving ourselves that we can embody the love of Christ for the world.

The Meditation

Allow yourself to take a moment to inhale and exhale. Imagine the early Christian communities facing harsh persecution—a constant, looming threat. Yet James urged them to remain faithful to Christ's teachings of justice and equality for all, particularly the marginalized. Exhale slowly, releasing any temptation to prioritize self-interest over communal well-being.

Inhale deeply once more. Consider how loving your neighbor as yourself isn't just about outward actions; it's also about fostering internal peace and recognizing your value. We often find it easier to show compassion to others than to ourselves. With each breath in, see yourself through God's eyes: worthy of love, respect, and care.

As you breathe out, think about the role of self-love in ministry. Valuing ourselves, we set a positive example for our congregations, demonstrating that everyone deserves love and kindness. It isn't vanity but a recognition of our intrinsic worth that enables us to serve others with a joyful heart.

Breathe in, absorbing the peace from self-acceptance, and breathe out. With each inhale and exhale, embrace self-love; with each exhale, extend that love to your congregation. This mutual understanding strengthens your community, uniting everyone in faith and love.

Remember, loving yourself isn't a diversion from your spiritual duties. It is a crucial part of fulfilling them. As you guide and nurture your flock, each step toward self-love is a step toward a more authentic ministry. Breathe in love for yourself, exhale, embodying Christ's love for the world.

The Questions
1. In moments of self-reflection, how do you perceive yourself through the lens of God's love? Do you extend the same compassion and understanding to yourself that you offer to your congregation?
2. How can you practice spiritual care to ensure you don't become spiritually or emotionally depleted?
3. What practical steps can you take to cultivate a sense of self-worth and well-being, and how can this enhance your ability to serve and connect with your community more effectively?

Chapter 5

Challenges

Matthew 9:35-10:8

We face constant turmoil and distress in these challenging times, bombarded by news of strife, sickness, and escalating global temperatures. It's as if the world itself is ablaze. It becomes difficult to discern God's gentle, guiding voice amid this chaos.

Imagine the weight of countless thoughts burdening your spirit with worry, clouding your vision of the future, prompting questions about purpose, and stirring a longing to find your place in this tumultuous world.

Reflect on the era of Jesus's ministry, a time of harsh Roman rule marked by poverty, political upheaval, and social fragmentation. The religious institutions of the day had grown complacent and stagnant, leading people away from God with rigid laws and rituals that burdened rather than uplifted their spirits. People craved to feel God's love and concern amid their oppression, which stifled their creativity and potential, leaving them leaderless and divided.

Despite these formidable challenges, Jesus embodied deep compassion for his people, preparing his disciples to venture into communities and address these dire needs. He equipped them with the

Holy Spirit's power, granting them the authority to heal, preach, and revitalize hope among the oppressed. This divine empowerment instilled in the disciples a fearless resolve to undertake Christ's mission, confidently confronting the injustices of their time.

This narrative holds profound implications for us today. As modern-day disciples, how do we respond to our community's needs with the same enthusiasm and commitment?

First, we must embody the compassion Jesus showed. Seeing the pain in our communities compels us to act—not out of obligation but moved by genuine empathy and concern. It is the first step in transforming our environment.

Second, preparation is crucial. Just as Jesus did not send his disciples unprepared, we, too, are equipped with knowledge, skills, and spiritual insights. These tools enable us to effectively minister and impact lives, relying on our deep engagement with the scriptures and communal worship practices.

Third, our focus must be local. While global concerns are significant, Jesus taught us the importance of addressing the needs within our immediate reach. It isn't about exclusion but prioritizing impact where we are most connected and where our efforts can be most effective.

Lastly, we are endowed with the same authority given to the disciples—to heal, uplift, and restore. With the Holy Spirit's power, we can speak life into despairing situations and bring healing and comfort to those who suffer.

Our faith community is a collective that shares the burden of ministry. We are interconnected, each vital to the other's spiritual wellbeing. This shared responsibility is our strength, enabling us to forge pathways of hope and renewal together. Let us embrace this call with zeal—working, praying, and walking in unity—empowered by the Holy Spirit to be the living embodiment of Christ's love on Earth.

The Meditation

As you sit quietly, take a deep breath. Inhale peace; exhale the turmoil of a world that seems aflame with strife, sickness, and rising temperatures. Feel the weight of these concerns lift with each breath, allowing space to hear God's gentle, guiding voice.

Inhale deeply again, envisioning the era of Jesus' ministry—a time riddled with poverty, political strife, and social division under harsh Roman rule. Exhale the heaviness of religious complacency and stagnant institutions that obscured the path to divine love and care. Imagine the people's longing for a sign of God's love amid their oppression.

Breathe in the spirit of deep compassion that Jesus embodied for his people, preparing his disciples to venture forth and meet these formidable challenges. With each exhale, release any fear, embracing the courage from the Holy Spirit's empowerment. Jesus gave his disciples the authority to heal, preach, and renew hope. They are gifts of power and resolve that you possess today.

Inhale, drawing in the knowledge and skills you've been blessed with, ready to engage deeply with scripture and community. Exhale, focus your efforts locally, and address the nearest needs, just as Jesus instructed his disciples to minister to the lost sheep of Israel.

Finally, breathe deeply and accept the shared responsibility of your faith community. Allow each inhale to remind you of the Holy Spirit's power within you—to heal, uplift, and restore. Each exhale is a commitment to act with compassion and unity, to forge paths of hope and renewal.

You are empowered to be the living embodiment of Christ's love on Earth. Embrace this mission with every breath, every action, every moment of quiet reflection.

As you open your eyes and return to the day that awaits, carry with you the serenity and strength from this time of reflection. You are prepared, empowered, and called. Step forward in faith, and let your actions speak of the love and commitment you've reaffirmed today.

The Questions

1. How can you cultivate a sense of compassion within yourself to better recognize and respond to the suffering in your community?

2. How can you effectively use your spiritual and practical resources to address your community's immediate needs while focusing on long-term transformation?
3. Reflect on the power of the Holy Spirit within you. How can you more actively engage this power to bring about healing and renewal in the environments you influence?

Chapter 6

Be Joyful

2 Samuel 6:12-15

Today, we encounter a poignant narrative centered around David, a celebrated king of Israel of East African descent. David's era was marked by struggles and profound victories, one of which involved the Ark of the Covenant—a sacred chest holding divine power and the laws given to Moses. This relic, which had once led Joshua through Canaan, symbolized the divine presence and was fiercely contested by the Philistines.

Despite its capture, the ark remained true to its purpose. Its presence among the Philistines brought turmoil, for it was not meant to dwell outside Israel. This disturbance was so profound that the Philistines, unable to bear its weight, returned it. This act reaffirms a vital truth: What is divinely ordained for you will find its way back, no matter the detours. It underscores that blessings intended for you will not flourish with another.

When David learned that the ark had been returned to Israel—safeguarded by Obed-Edom, a Levite, and brought blessings to his household—he was moved to reclaim it for himself and all his people. The joy that filled David upon reclaiming the ark was uncontainable, manifesting in a spirited dance.

His actions were not just a celebration of retrieval but a profound acknowledgment of the restoration of divine favor and empowerment to his people and land.

David's joy was not superficial. It was a sincere reflection of his faith and foresight. He saw beyond the immediate joy of the ark's return; he envisioned the reactivation of divine blessings and power. His happiness was a testament to the inner peace and assurance of knowing divine favor is at work.

David's expression of joy teaches us that true happiness is more than a fleeting emotion; it is a state of being, a constant in the lives of those who feel the presence of the divine. This joy, deeply rooted in divine assurance, allows no room for despair or feelings of unworthiness. It is a powerful force that banishes doubt and nurtures a spirit resilient against the trials of life.

Choosing joy is an active, daily decision to see beyond current struggles and anticipate the blessings that lie ahead. It acknowledges the presence of the divine in every aspect of life, understanding that every challenge is an opportunity for growth and every victory a chance to give thanks.

The story of David and the ark invites us to lead with joy and inspire our communities to recognize and rejoice in the divine presence among us. It calls us to encourage each other to dance in the face of challenges, sing as we move through trials, and remain steadfast in the joy that comes from faith.

Every sanctuary, sacred space, and moment of worship can be a channel of joy. We can uplift ourselves and those we lead, creating ripples of positivity and faith that transform lives.

As we reflect on our journeys, the spirit of joy can be our guide and strength. We can dance like David, with hearts unburdened and spirits uplifted, as we embrace the divine blessings that await us. This joy is our heritage and strength, guiding us through the darkest nights to the brightest mornings.

Breathe and allow yourself to be open to profound joy.

The Meditation

Take a moment to find a quiet space. Sit comfortably, close your eyes, and take a deep breath in. Exhale slowly, feeling the weight of your daily responsibilities lift with each breath out. As you settle into this space, reflect on the story of David and the Ark of the Covenant—a tale of endurance and divine presence through struggles and triumphs.

Inhale deeply, drawing in the resilience and faith that David demonstrated. As you breathe, consider the sacred chest that once led Joshua through Canaan, fiercely contested yet unyielding in its purpose. As you exhale, release the turmoil it caused among the Philistines, a reminder that what is yours will return despite the challenges it may face.

With another inhale, envision the ark returning to Israel, to Obed-Edom's care, and the blessings it brought to his household. Imagine David's surge of joy as he danced in a spirit of thanks. This joy was not just for the moment but a deep, resonant recognition of divine favor restored.

Breathe in this joy, allowing it to fill you from within, strengthening your faith and foresight. With each exhale, let go of any doubts or feelings of unworthiness. Allow this practice of breathing to anchor you in the present, reminding you of the continuous presence of the divine in your life.

Continue to breathe deeply, absorbing the strength and assurance from divine blessings. As you exhale, imagine imparting this joy to your congregation, inspiring them through your leadership and faith. Let this meditation empower you to face challenges with a joyful heart and a steadfast spirit.

As you conclude this time of reflection, take a few more deep breaths. With each inhale, draw in peace and positivity. With each exhale, release anything that does not serve your spirit.

Gently open your eyes, carrying the joy and strength of David with you, ready to lead and uplift those around you with a renewed sense of purpose and joy.

The Questions
1. In moments of challenge, how can you more consciously choose joy over despair, remembering David's example of embracing joy even before seeing the fulfillment of God's promises?
2. Reflect on when something important was returned to you, whether it was an opportunity, a relationship, or a sense of peace. How did you recognize it as a divine intervention in your life?
3. How can you cultivate gratitude and joy that uplifts your spirit and inspires those around you, transforming challenges into opportunities for growth and celebration?

Chapter 7

Divine Possibilities

John 14:10-13

Prayer is more than a daily routine or a solemn tradition. It serves as a lifeline, a quiet moment of intimacy in a bustling world where the clamor of our duties can drown out the inner peace we crave. In daily prayer, we find our minds calmed, our souls comforted, and our bodies relaxed. Prayer empowers the spirit and fortifies the heart to face life's many challenges with courage. Yet prayer's significance extends beyond the personal; it is inherently tied to our collective mission as followers of Christ. Prayer opens our eyes to divine possibilities, a theme vividly explored in today's scripture, where Jesus discusses these possibilities with his disciples.

Many overlook the depth of Jesus's words, perhaps because of their perceived impracticality. It's common to hear believers express a wish for the miraculous powers of Christ—to raise the dead, calm storms, or heal the incurable. However, these desires miss the broader message. Jesus was endowed with unique powers, gifts, and graces, but scripture also reassures us that we have been equipped with gifts and graces, perhaps even capable of exceeding those of Christ in our context. Understanding Jesus's message requires thoroughly examining his words and the circumstances surrounding them.

In his dialogue, Jesus was not merely forecasting his death and resurrection but preparing his disciples for the trials ahead. He promised the coming of the Holy Spirit—a comforter to guide, empower, and sustain them in his absence. This Holy Spirit is not just a transient presence but a constant companion that reinforces us amid life's storms, lightens our burdens, and infuses strength during our weakest moments. Jesus's proclamation, "greater works than these shall you do," was not a call to replicate his miracles but an assurance that the Holy Spirit would enable us to fulfill our God-given missions.

The essence of Jesus's statement, "greater works will you do," becomes more apparent through its original Greek meaning. The term "work" (érgon) suggests not just action but a profound purpose and desire to impact lives and expand God's kingdom. When we align ourselves with Jesus's teachings, the Holy Spirit awakens us to these divine possibilities—opportunities to accomplish the extraordinary tasks for which we were created. This Spirit instills in us a deep-seated desire to serve purposefully, ensuring our endeavors inspire others to lead more fulfilling lives.

Consider, for example, the divine call to create, whether crafting a poem, singing a song, or speaking with conviction. Through the Holy Spirit, these acts transcend mere performance; they become transformative, encouraging others to improve, extend kindness, and embrace God's grace. This transformation is the "greater work" — using our divine gifts competently and with profound impact.

The story of Mary McCloud Bethune illustrates this beautifully. Inspired by the Holy Spirit, she envisioned and founded a school on what others saw as vacant land. She didn't perform visible miracles, but she created something lasting—an institution that continues to educate and empower.

So how do we embark on these greater works? It begins by cultivating a deep, personal connection with the Holy Spirit, making ourselves receptive to this divine influence. We must also embrace submission to the Spirit's guidance, which can be challenging as it requires vulnerability and relinquishing control. Moreover, we need to depend not on human wisdom or strength but on the reliability and assurance the Holy Spirit provides. Finally, setting aside our egos allows us to be conduits of the Spirit's power, focusing not on self-promotion but on serving others.

As we continue in our ministries, we engage the power of prayer and the guidance of the Holy Spirit. Embrace the divine possibilities God has laid before us, carrying forward the work of Christ in unity and faith.

The Meditation

Take a moment to pause and breathe deeply. Inhale slowly, feeling the air fill your lungs, bringing quiet to the mind and peace to the soul. As you exhale, let go of the day's burdens and the clamor that disrupts your serenity. This practice of breathing is your prayer—a vital connection to the divine, not just routine but a profound communion in your bustling life.

With each breath, remember the gifts and graces you possess, as affirmed by scripture. These are not just for personal edification but align you with Christ's mission, opening your eyes to what might seem impossible. Today, reflect on Jesus's words about the divine possibilities available to us, his followers, through the Holy Spirit.

As you breathe in, invite the Holy Spirit to fill you with strength and courage for the trials ahead. As you breathe out, release any doubt, trusting in the promise that "greater works than these shall you do," enabled not by our power but through the Holy Spirit.

Inhale the desire to impact lives and expand God's kingdom. Exhale the hesitation that hinders your divine calling. Let this rhythm of breathing guide you to align deeper with Jesus's teachings and awaken to the extraordinary tasks you are created to accomplish.

Imagine the Holy Spirit as a constant companion, infusing every word you speak, every song you sing, and every poem you write with transformative power. Each creative act becomes a greater work, not just in performance but in purpose, inspiring others to embrace a more fulfilling life.

Reflect on the story of Mary McCloud Bethune as you breathe. Inspired by the Holy Spirit, she saw beyond vacant land to a future of education and empowerment. Inhale her vision; exhale any limitations.

To embrace these works, cultivate a personal connection with the Holy Spirit. Allow each inhale to draw in divine guidance and exhale to surrender your will. Depend on this spiritual relationship, letting go of self-reliance and embracing divine assurance.

As you continue this meditative breathing, remember the power of prayer and the guidance of the Holy Spirit. Embrace the divine possibilities laid before you, carrying forward the work of Christ in unity and faith.

The Questions

1. How can you integrate the practice of inviting the Holy Spirit into your daily moments of prayer and reflection to better recognize and act upon the divine possibilities presented to you?
2. How have you witnessed the transformation of your gifts and graces when aligned with the Holy Spirit's power? In what specific situations have you felt this divine influence guiding your actions toward greater works?
3. Reflecting on the story of Mary McCloud Bethune and her vision for what others saw as vacant land, consider what "vacant lands" exist in your community or ministry that, with divine inspiration, could be transformed into sources of growth and empowerment?

Chapter 8

Plan Your Next Victory

Joshua 1:7-9 and 3:1-9

Joshua was a warrior. He dedicated himself to securing victories for Israel, excelling in his dedication far beyond others. His life unfolded amid people who had spent years aimlessly wandering the Egyptian desert. These people, who had strayed from the path to the land their ancestors had left more than four centuries ago, were united only in their indecision and fear. Though Moses freed them from captivity in Egypt, their stubbornness, shortsightedness, and fear kept them from entering the land promised to Abraham.

Their reluctance was rooted in comfort with the familiar wilderness, leading to a refusal to trust and embrace the future. This resistance to change meant that an entire generation missed the opportunity to claim their inheritance, leaving them to wander until a new generation ready for change arose.

This narrative reflects a broader, timeless issue: the hindrance of progress by those too comfortable in their positions to foster growth or pass on wisdom. In our communities today, we see similar patterns. Long-tenured leaders in various sectors, including politics, often resist the evolution of leadership, clinging to power rather than preparing the next generation to lead. This stalls progress and denies young, energetic leaders the chance to bring fresh perspectives and innovations.

The reluctance to evolve leadership was also evident in the aftermath of the civil rights movement. The movement saw significant victories but failed in some respects to equip the next generation with the leadership and survival skills necessary to continue the fight against enduring injustices like racism and inequality.

Joshua's story diverges here. Encouraged by Moses to be strong and courageous, Joshua represented a readiness to embrace God's promise. He and his contemporaries were prepared to lead their people into the Promised Land, signaling a shift from the stagnation of the past to the promise of a fruitful future.

God's command to Joshua to adhere strictly to the Torah illustrates the importance of grounding leadership in wisdom and ethical guidelines. By meditating on and adhering to these principles, Joshua was prepared to lead and win. As the old guard made way, Joshua's new strategies and fearless approach allowed him to succeed where the previous generation had faltered.

Similar principles apply to our personal, societal, or global struggles. We face numerous battles against pandemics, divisive politics, and social injustices. Yet just as God guided Joshua, we, too, can find guidance through faith, community, and the wisdom of scripture.

Our battles require that we learn to focus on victory rather than obstacles. The Israelites feared the giants in Canaan, but Joshua saw past the immediate threats to the promise of victory. In our lives, too, focusing on past successes can provide the courage to face current challenges.

Surrounding ourselves with positive, supportive people is vital. Negative influences can trap us in a cycle of fear and defeat, whereas supportive communities uplift us and remind us of our strengths and the promises of our faith.

Finally, reflecting on our past victories helps us see beyond our struggles. Joshua didn't focus on the power of his adversaries; he saw the victory awaiting him, promised by God. Similarly, we must focus on the assurance of our faith that we are never alone in our battles and victory is possible.

As you face new challenges, remember you are a warrior of wisdom, equipped by your faith to overcome whatever stands before you. So plan your next victory.

The Meditation

Take a moment to center yourself in quiet reflection. As you sit comfortably, close your eyes, and begin to inhale deeply and exhale slowly, releasing the tensions of the day. With each breath, allow yourself to become more present in this moment, more aware of the stillness within you.

Inhale deeply and consider the journey of Joshua, a leader who emerged from a generation lost in the wilderness, surrounded by fear and indecision. Exhale slowly, releasing any feelings of resistance and reluctance.

Breathe in, drawing in the strength and dedication of Joshua, who excelled in securing victories by trusting in divine promises. As you exhale, let go of any hesitation that hinders your path to embrace the future with courage.

With each breath, think about the stagnation caused by clinging to the past, as seen in the wilderness wanderers and today's leaders who may resist passing wisdom and opportunities to the next generation. Inhale the possibility of change, and exhale the comfort of the familiar, clearing a path for growth and innovation in your leadership.

As you breathe deeply, meditate on the scripture and its wisdom. Allow the words to guide you, infusing your spirit with the strength to lead and care for others.

Inhale the vision of the Promised Land—a place of peace and prosperity that awaits beyond current challenges. Exhale any fear of the giants that may appear along your journey, focusing instead on the victories ahead.

Surround yourself with thoughts of supportive and uplifting community members as you breathe in. Exhale to release negativity and doubt, reinforcing your foundation in faith and community.

Finally, as you prepare to open your eyes, inhale confidence and a renewed sense of purpose. Exhale and embrace the role of a warrior of wisdom, equipped and ready to face whatever comes your way with a steadfast heart and an unyielding spirit.

Remember, you are never alone in your battles; like Joshua, you are supported by a promise of victory. Let this meditation strengthen your resolve to lead with courage and integrity, planning your next victory.

The Questions

1. What fears or hesitations are holding you back from embracing new opportunities or changes in your life and leadership?
2. How can you pass on your knowledge and experience more effectively to empower the next generation of leaders?
3. How can you strengthen your faith and community connections to better support you in overcoming your challenges?

Chapter 9

When You Feel Invisible

Mark 5:25-34

Today, in Mark's Gospel, a narrative unfolds about a woman, unnamed and unnoticed. She grapples with a condition that not only causes her physical pain but also societal exile. For twelve years, she endures not just the physical ailment of relentless bleeding but the harsh judgment of her community, deeming her unclean according to their purity laws. This woman, isolated and marginalized, becomes a poignant emblem of invisibility, her presence almost erased beneath the weight of cultural decrees and medical despair.

Imagine her world, sharply defined by barriers society created where touching another person or even an object could amplify her isolation. Her condition renders her untouchable, unworthy in the eyes of her society, and perhaps, in the darkest moments, even in her own eyes.

Yet amid this backdrop of suffering and solitude, she hears of Jesus—a figure of healing and hope. Despite the social constraints and personal fears, she resolves to seek him out. Picture her weaving through the crowded streets, driven by desperation and determination, focused on touching the hem of his garment. This act isn't a mere brush against fabric; it's an intentional, firm grasp born of a belief in the possibility of healing and recognition.

When Jesus acknowledges her—calling her "daughter" and affirming her faith—he does more than heal her physically; he restores her dignity and redefines her identity. No longer invisible, she is recognized, seen, and validated in her community and the realm of faith.

There may be moments when you, too, feel invisible, your efforts unseen, your struggles unnoticed. The journey can be disheartening when the impact of your work isn't apparent or the acknowledgment you hope for doesn't materialize. Yet like the woman in the story, your worth and calling transcend the immediate recognition of those around you.

This narrative invites you to consider the barriers that may make you feel isolated or undervalued—whether they stem from within your perceptions or from the expectations and judgments of others. It encourages reflection on the deeper sources of validation and the true essence of your ministry.

As shown through Christ's response to the woman, the power of God offers a profound reminder: You are never truly invisible. You are seen, you are known, and you are valued beyond the confines of human acknowledgment. The very essence of your faith and determination can guide you to transcend the barriers that may seem impossible to overcome.

Moreover, the story is a call to action. It challenges you to reach out, persist, and engage deeply with the divine power that sustains and empowers you. Just as the woman overcame her obstacles to touch the garment of Jesus, you, too, are invited to cling to the principles and promises of your faith—allowing them to heal, renew, and affirm your purpose.

Allow the garment to symbolize Christ's teachings: love, peace, courage, self-forgiveness, and a divine plan for your life. Embrace these garments. Let them clothe you in strength and visibility, ensuring you are restored to wholeness and can find your place and peace within the vast family of God.

Hold onto these truths with urgency and persistence. Your challenges and your unseen battles are known to God. In the grand tapestry of divine work, every thread—visible or not—is crucial to the integrity and beauty of the whole. In your hands, even the unseen becomes a vital part of the spiritual landscape, touching lives and shaping destinies in ways you may never fully see but that are known and cherished by God.

The Meditation

Sit comfortably, close your eyes, and take a deep breath. Inhale slowly, feeling the air fill your lungs, and as you exhale, let go of the burdens and expectations placed upon you. With each breath, imagine the world of a woman from Mark's Gospel, unnamed and often unseen, carrying the weight of societal judgment and physical affliction for twelve long years. Inhale compassion for her struggles and exhale any feelings of invisibility or isolation you might share with her.

As you breathe in, envision her courage as she hears of Jesus, a source of healing and hope. With each exhale, release the fear and constraints that hold you back. Picture her determination, weaving through crowded streets, focused solely on touching the hem of Jesus's garment. Breathe in her resolve, and as you exhale, let go of doubts.

With your next inhalation, draw in the moment Jesus acknowledges her—calling her "daughter" and affirming her faith. Feel the power of being seen and recognized. Exhale and let go of the invisibility that sometimes shadows your work and efforts. Remember, as she was restored, you, too, are recognized and valued beyond the immediate acknowledgment of those around you.

Continue to breathe deeply. With each breath, contemplate the barriers you face—whether from external expectations or internal fears. Inhale the strength to confront these barriers and exhale the limitations they impose upon you.

As you breathe, cling to the teachings of Christ like the woman clung to his garment. Inhale the love, peace, and courage that these teachings offer. Exhale and embrace the renewal and affirmation of your purpose. Feel the garment of Christ's teachings clothe you in strength and visibility.

Now gently bring your focus back to the present. Take one last deep breath, feeling the connection to the divine power that sees, knows, and cherishes you. Slowly open your eyes, refreshed and reassured that no effort is unseen in your ministry, and no struggle is unnoticed. Hold onto this truth with urgency and persistence, allowing it to transform and heal you as you continue to touch lives and fulfill your calling.

The Questions
1. Reflect on when you felt unseen or unacknowledged in your ministry. How did you navigate these feelings, and what could you learn from the woman's story about seeking recognition and healing despite societal barriers?
2. Consider the moment the woman reaches out and touches Jesus's garment. What barriers (physical, emotional, or spiritual) are you currently facing that require a similar act of courage and faith? How can you actively seek to overcome these obstacles in your ministry?
3. Think about how you seek healing and restoration for yourself while you serve others. How can the idea of "clinging to the garment" or embracing the teachings of Christ help you find peace and strength in times of personal or professional turmoil?

Chapter 10

Breathe

Genesis 2:5-7

Consider for a moment the act of breathing. This fundamental process, effortless and continuous, is often overlooked daily. We breathe in and out without a second thought, whether awake or asleep, calm or under stress. Yet there's a profound lesson hidden in this simple act for those of us who guide and nurture others.

The Genesis account of creation vividly illustrates the first human being coming to life through divine breath. When the Creator breathed into the newly formed figure of dust, that figure didn't just start to breathe; it became a living soul. This narrative isn't just a tale of origins but a profound affirmation of the sanctity and potential within each breath we take.

The breath bestowed upon us is not merely biological. It's a sacred infusion, a gift that animates our physical being and empowers our spiritual essence. This breath is no ordinary wind; it is the essence of life itself, divine and pulsating with potential. It reminds us that our humanity is deeply connected to the divine and that our existence hinges on something sacred and powerful.

Consider how often we're advised to "take a deep breath" in moments of crisis or anxiety. It isn't just about calming our nerves; it's a call to reconnect with that original gift of life—the breath of soul power. This soul power is our heritage, a strength that enables us to endure, persist, and prevail against the odds.

Yet hostile forces seem intent on diminishing this divine spark. We face challenges and adversities designed to drain our spirit and divert our purpose. Individuals and systems may try to label us, reduce us to categories, or diminish our value. They manipulate, coerce, and strive to make us forget our inherent worth and the power vested in us.

But we must remember the breath of life that animates us. We are made in the divine image, equipped with creativity and agency. We possess the ability to define ourselves and our surroundings. Like the first human in the garden, we have the authority to name and shape our reality.

When the world around you attempts to dictate your identity or your path, recall that original breath. Remind yourself that you were created to be a cocreator, to work wonders with the life force within you. You have the strength to confront negativity and transform it into something positive.

So when life challenges you, when you find yourself up against insurmountable barriers, return to the essence of your creation. Breathe deeply. Harness your soul power. Engage with the world not as a victim but as a vital force of love, joy, peace, and creativity. Each breath you take is a reaffirmation of your purpose and your potential to effect change.

Inhale deeply the love that surrounds you; exhale joy into the world. Inhale peace that surpasses understanding; exhale serenity into the chaos. Inhale the strength from your deepest reserves; exhale power into your actions. Breathe in courage and breathe out accomplishments. Embrace faith and release determination.

The breath of life is not just a physiological necessity but the rhythm of the divine in us. It reminds us of our incredible soul power, shaping destinies and inspiring generations. Let us live fully aware of this power, embracing and embodying the love of the Creator in every breath we take.

The Meditation

Take a moment to focus on breathing, a natural and continuous process that often goes unnoticed. This simple act holds profound significance, particularly for those who guide and care for others.

In the Genesis creation narrative, the breath of life transforms dust into a living soul. This breath is no ordinary air; it's a divine infusion that animates our physical bodies and elevates our spiritual essence, connecting our humanity to the sacred.

As you face daily stresses or moments of decision, remember the importance of deep, mindful breathing. Each inhale draws in more than just air; it pulls in the sacred life force that revitalizes and empowers you. Each exhale does more than release carbon dioxide; it dispels worries and refreshes your spirit.

When external pressures seek to diminish your light or when others attempt to define your worth, recall that you are imbued with this divine breath. You are made in the image of the Creator, endowed with creativity and the ability to shape your environment and express your inherent gifts.

Focus on each breath to engage in mindful breathing. Inhale deeply, letting the air fill you with love and peace. Exhale slowly, releasing joy and serenity into your surroundings. Let each breath in draw strength from the deepest places within you, and let each breath out channel that strength into positive, decisive actions. Embrace courage as you breathe in, and let go of fear as you breathe out.

This rhythmic breathing transcends physical necessity and reveals our divine presence. It is a constant reminder of the incredible power we hold.

Let this practice reaffirm your purpose and enhance your capacity to bring about change. Embrace and embody the divine rhythm in every breath, fully aware of the soul power that shapes destinies and ignites hope.

The Questions

1. How does your understanding of breath as a divine gift influ-

ence your perspective on everyday challenges and interactions?
2. How can mindful breathing help you reconnect with your core values and sense of purpose in moments of stress or uncertainty?
3. What practical ways can you remind yourself daily of your inherent soul power and the creative potential that resides within you?

Chapter 11

Choices

Psalm 16

In today's scripture reading, we reflect on King David, hailed as one of Israel's most esteemed rulers. He was a fierce warrior who faced numerous battles on the field and within his spirit. Interestingly, even a figure as formidable as David begins his psalm with a plea for sanctuary, saying, "Protect me, O God, for in you I take refuge." It's a potent reminder of the vulnerability that resides even in the mightiest among us.

David's life was shadowed by King Saul's envy, driven by his knowledge that while the people chose him, God anointed David. This divine choice did not shield David from peril but marked him for a great, though arduous, destiny. Saul's jealousy led him to pursue David relentlessly, and he was determined to prevent him from ascending to the throne that was rightfully his. This narrative underscores a poignant truth: Being chosen by God to fulfill a purpose, no matter its magnitude, does not guarantee universal acceptance or ease.

Saul's pursuit of David with a vast army highlights a stark imbalance of power—three thousand against David's four hundred. Yet David's connection with God, being "a man after God's own heart," signifies a profound mutual choice between David and the divine—a relationship rooted in trust and commitment.

This relationship did not exempt David from fear or danger. His life was not a tranquil journey devoid of threats. Despite his courage and prowess, there were moments when he found himself desperately outnumbered and cried out for divine protection. Saul even tried to sever David's spiritual ties, urging him to forsake his faith and seek other gods. But David's faith in the God of Israel was unshakable; he knew no other deity could offer him the protection and blessings he received from God.

David's trials mirror our own as we navigate leadership and spirituality in a complex world. The apostle Paul reminds us to put on the whole armor of God, not merely as a defense mechanism but as a continual connection to our divine leader, ensuring Christ remains central in our lives.

In our busy lives, where distractions abound, it is crucial to pause and reflect. Has the pursuit of material success, personal relationships, or even daily responsibilities begun to overshadow our spiritual commitments? Do these pursuits drain us of the energy to engage with the divine at the day's start or end?

In a world where many voices and influences beckon us toward secular gods—materialism, entertainment, fame—it's vital to remember the essence of our faith. Like David, we must affirm our choice in God, recognizing the blessings and divine grace that guide us to a life of abundance and purpose.

As you reflect on your path today, consider whether Christ remains your cornerstone, your first choice in every endeavor and challenge. In affirming this choice lies the power to transcend trials and embody the light we are called to be in the world.

So let us rejoice in this calling and continue to walk boldly in the light of Christ, for in doing so, we fulfill our highest calling and most profound purpose.

The Meditation

As you enter into a mindful meditation today, draw inspiration from the life of King David, whose vulnerability was expressed in his heartfelt plea: "Protect me, O God, for in you I take refuge."

Begin by finding a quiet space. Sit comfortably, close your eyes, and take a deep breath in. Exhale slowly, feeling any tension melt away. Inhale, imagining yourself drawing in peace and stillness. Exhale, releasing the burdens and distractions that cloud your mind.

Reflect on David's story. Despite his power and the divine favor he enjoyed, David faced immense challenges and felt profound fear. Breathe in deeply and consider the pressures you face in your own life. Exhale and let go of the need for control and the fear of judgment.

Inhale and remember David's steadfast faith, even when Saul's envy drove him to pursue David with overwhelming force. Think about your relationship with the divine. Exhale any doubts, reaffirming your trust and commitment.

With each breath, contemplate the imbalance David faced—outnumbered yet unshaken. Inhale strength, acknowledging that, like David, you are not alone. God's presence is with you. Exhale and release feelings of isolation or inadequacy.

As you breathe deeply, consider how external demands can distract from spiritual commitments. Inhale, calling to mind the essence of your faith and the armor of God that shields you. Exhale, letting go of the material pursuits and distractions that compete for your attention.

Finally, breathe in and ask yourself if Christ remains the cornerstone of your life. With each exhale, release anything that competes with this central relationship.

Remember your connection to the living Christ within and the path before you. Breathe in confidence and exhale with gratitude. As you slowly open your eyes, carry this sense of purpose and peace with you, ready to face the world's challenges with a renewed spirit and a steadfast heart.

The Questions

1. In moments of challenge or fear, how can you more actively

seek refuge and strength in your faith, similar to how David did in his time of peril?
2. Reflecting on your daily activities and responsibilities, what specific practices or habits can you implement to ensure that your spiritual commitments remain a priority amid life's distractions?
3. How does the story of David's unwavering faith despite opposition inspire you to handle the external pressures and influences that threaten to diminish your spiritual focus?

Chapter 12

Don't Be Afraid to Fail

Acts 15:36-40

Chadwick Boseman, born in the quiet town of Anderson, South Carolina, exemplifies a story of perseverance and courage that resonates deeply with the lives of many, including those who serve in ministry. Before he graced the world stage as a celebrated actor, Boseman was a high school junior staging his first play. This early glimpse of his storytelling prowess was only the beginning. As he matured into his roles at Howard University and later on the global cinema stage, his life illustrated that outstanding achievements often come from humble beginnings and are fraught with setbacks and delays.

Boseman didn't land his breakout role as Jackie Robinson in *42* until he was thirty-five, and he was forty when he brought T'Challa to life in *Black Panther*. These milestones, significant as they are, do not fully encapsulate the essence of his impact. Boseman's true strength was in his unyielding resolve to press forward, regardless of the obstacles he faced or the delays in achieving his dreams. He became a symbol of heroism not just through his roles but also through his life, characterized by an inspiring fearlessness in the face of failure.

This reflection on Boseman's journey offers a powerful example of the meaning of patience. We may have moments of public success and private struggles. Like Boseman and his acting career, we often face long periods of waiting, seasons of doubt, and experiences of failure before witnessing the fruits of our labor in our communities.

In our culture, failure is often seen as a final, embarrassing stain rather than a step in the process. Yet the biblical narratives tell a different story—Joshua, Samson, and Peter experienced significant failures. Joshua faced military defeat, Samson succumbed to betrayal and personal failure, and Peter denied Christ at a crucial moment. However, these were not their end stories. Each found redemption and a renewed path forward, showing us that failure is a part of the human experience, integral to spiritual and personal growth.

Similarly, the story of John Mark in the New Testament reflects the journey of many who falter in their first steps, only to rise stronger. Initially failing to stick with Paul and Barnabas on a missionary journey, Mark eventually matures into a figure of strength and reliability, one whom even Paul later regards as valuable to his ministry. Mark's story is particularly poignant for young people and leaders, demonstrating that early failures do not dictate our final contributions.

Embracing our vulnerabilities and failures can be transformative. For instance, during Advent, we are reminded that every Advent is an opportunity to prepare our hearts anew for the indwelling of divine grace and let the light of Christ transform our weaknesses into strengths. In our failures, we often find the most profound lessons and the strongest motivations to pursue our calling with renewed vigor and faith.

Let us embrace the failures that are part of our growth. Let us allow these experiences to refine us and not define us. Encourage your congregation to see each setback as an opportunity to let the light of Christ shine through them more brightly, guiding them to resilience and renewal.

In this reflection, remember that our moments of waiting and experiences of failure may seem like delays but are essential chapters in our stories of faith and perseverance. These stories are to be shared, providing hope and encouragement to others that even through failures, with faith, we continue to move forward, building a legacy of courage and commitment in the light of Christ's eternal love.

The Meditation

Take a moment to settle into a comfortable position.

Close your eyes, take a deep breath in, and slowly exhale. Let your body relax with each breath, releasing tension as you prepare your heart and mind for reflection and meditation.

As you continue to breathe deeply, inhale peace and exhale any stress or distractions. Consider the story of Chadwick Boseman, whose life journey resonates deeply with the essence of perseverance and courage. Born in a quiet town and beginning his creative path early in life, he faced many years of uncertainty and setbacks before achieving remarkable success.

With each breath, consider the times you have faced delays or difficulties. Inhale deeply, acknowledge these challenges, and exhale, releasing the burden they may carry. Like Boseman, you, too, have moments of waiting and seasons of doubt, yet these are not in vain. They are part of a larger story, shaping you into the leader you are meant to become.

Breathe in the stories of biblical figures like Joshua, Samson, and Peter—each faced significant failures yet found redemption and a path forward. Allow their stories to fill you with hope and the reassurance that failure is a part of the human and spiritual journey, not the end of it.

As you inhale, imagine drawing in strength and resilience. As you exhale, let go of any fear of failure. Think of John Mark, who faltered early but grew into a figure of strength and reliability. His journey reminds us that our early setbacks do not determine our final impact.

Continue to breathe deeply, and with each breath, embrace your vulnerabilities and past failures, letting them transform under the light of Christ. These experiences refine us, teaching us profound lessons and motivating us to press forward with renewed faith and vigor.

As you prepare to open your eyes and return to your day, carry with you the reminder of Boseman's legacy—not merely as an actor but as a symbol of fearlessness in the face of adversity. Let his story, and those of biblical characters, inspire you to view each moment of failure not as a setback but as a vital chapter in your own story of faith and perseverance.

With one last deep breath in and a slow exhale, open your eyes, refreshed and renewed, ready to let the light of Christ shine brightly through you, guiding you to resilience and renewal.

The Questions
1. What personal setbacks or failures have you experienced in your ministry or life that initially seemed challenging? How did these experiences contribute to your growth and understanding of your calling?
2. Reflect on a time when you witnessed resilience, either in yourself or someone else, in the face of challenges. What lessons did you learn about faith and perseverance from this experience?
3. As you consider the stories of biblical figures like Joshua, Samson, Peter, and John Mark, which aspects of their journeys resonate most with you right now? How can their experiences of redemption and renewal inspire your approach to leadership and personal setbacks?

Chapter 13

Blessings

1 Chronicles 16: 8-10, 34-36

In the rhythm of daily responsibilities and challenges, it's easy to overlook the connection between physical health and spiritual disposition. Recent insights from the field of nutrition suggest that our mental state can influence our overall health as significantly as our diet. A positive attitude may contribute to a stronger immune system, helping to ward off illness. It's a stirring reminder: The health of our bodies is intricately linked to the joy and optimism we harbor within.

Our bodies, though complex, respond in straightforward ways. They cannot decipher the source of stress or anxiety; they react to perceived threats. This reaction often manifests as inflammation, which is at the root of many health issues, such as diabetes, heart disease, and depression. Anxiety about future uncertainties or the amplification of minor worries into crises can provoke this physical response, leading to physical ailments.

Reflecting on these insights, it becomes clear that fostering an attitude of optimism and gratitude is not just beneficial; it's essential. This perspective echoes throughout spiritual teachings and is vividly captured in David's experience following the return of the Ark of the

Covenant to Jerusalem. David's spontaneous dance of joy and gratitude illustrates a profound truth: When we place divine love at the center of our lives, gratitude flows naturally.

1 Chronicles 16 offers profound lessons on gratitude that are especially resonant for our ministry. The scripture encourages us to express our thankfulness openly. It suggests that gratitude should be a daily practice, not confined to particular moments or celebrations. Indeed, transforming gratitude into a lifestyle enriches our lives and inspires those around us. As we express our thanks, we are reminded of God's unwavering presence and love, which sustain us through all trials.

Moreover, our gratitude should be shared publicly. It serves as a counter narrative to the prevalent voices of discontent and despair in the world. In a society where many amplify negativity and conflict, our call is to affirm God's goodness, celebrate divine grace, and articulate the positive transformations we witness. By doing so, we uplift others and fortify our spiritual journey.

Gratitude, therefore, is not just an emotional response but a transformative force. It enables us to perceive the divine even in dark times, to connect more deeply with our community, and to live out our faith more fully. As we express our thankfulness, we embrace the spiritual practice of gratitude.

We count our blessings and continually reflect on what we have rather than our lack. This practice isn't just an exercise in positive thinking; it's a way to align more closely with the divine, promoting spiritual well-being and physical health. Let gratitude be the lens through which we view our life's journey, enhancing our perception of the world and deepening our connection with the divine.

In cultivating a heart of thankfulness, we realize gratitude is a response to goodness and our foundational attitude toward life.

The Meditation

Find a quiet spot where you can sit comfortably. Close your eyes and take a deep breath. Slowly inhale, feeling the air nourish your body and bring life. As you exhale, gently let go of any stress and worries that weigh on your mind and heart.

Reflect on how joy, optimism, and gratitude can uplift your spirits and boost your physical health. Stress and anxiety can trigger physical reactions like inflammation, which might lead to more severe health issues. By focusing on positive thoughts, you're positively affecting your body's health.

Keep breathing deeply. Think about David who, filled with joy and thankfulness after the return of the ark, danced before God. His gratitude was a powerful acknowledgment of God's presence and blessings. Let this story inspire you to express gratitude in your life, visibly and vibrantly, every day.

With each breath in, draw in positivity and peace. With each breath out, release negativity and stress. Fill your mind with thoughts of gratitude. Consider the blessings, successes, and even challenges in your life as each has shaped you and brought you closer to the divine.

Make this meditation a regular part of your daily routine. Each session is a chance to align more closely with divine love, overcome difficulties, and appreciate the abundance around you. Gratitude is transformative—it changes how you see your circumstances, enriching your interaction with the world and deepening your faith.

As you finish your meditation, open your eyes with a renewed sense of peace and purpose. Let this sense of thankfulness guide your actions and interactions. Remember, living with gratitude benefits your spiritual health and whole being, creating a holistic harmony that supports you in all you do.

The Questions

1. In what ways have you noticed your physical health being affected by your mental and emotional state? Reflect on specific instances where a change in your attitude or emotional response has made a noticeable difference in your physical well-being.
2. How can you more actively incorporate gratitude into your

daily life and ministry? Consider practical steps to make gratitude a more visible and consistent practice in your personal and professional interactions.
3. Reflect on the story of David and the Ark of the Covenant. What can this Scripture teach you about the impact of public expressions of gratitude on your community and those you lead? How might you inspire others to embrace a lifestyle of gratitude through your actions and words?

Chapter 14

What Is Required?

Micah 6:1-8

In the stirring echoes of the prophet Micah's narrative, we encounter a vivid recount of a people profoundly bound in their journey with the divine, transitioning from chains to liberation, despair to hope, and oppression to justice. Micah succinctly traces the inception of Israel's covenant with the sacred—a pact laden with expectations and a clear call to a life of obedience and reverence.

This tale is not just historical; it serves as a mirror reflecting our own experiences. It's a call to remember and act upon the divine's expectations. The prophets, like sentinels, stood to warn and urge a people comfortable under the protective wing of the divine yet often straying into complacency and rebellion.

Yet history tells us of the struggle to meet these divine expectations. Israel often resorted to rituals and offerings—substitutes for the genuine justice, mercy, and humility required. They stood at a crossroads time and again, as do our communities and congregations today. We, too, have witnessed divine intervention in our darkest times, yet we find the divine mandate challenging to uphold.

Micah's words are not just a recounting of failings but a clarion call to remember and renew our commitment. The narrative highlights a dispute, a broken covenant because of Israel's failures—a reminder that the relationship demands fidelity, not merely sacrifice or ritual.

Through Micah, God asks, "What has been done to you, Israel?" The question is touching because God remembers the covenant, but the people fail to honor it. The answer can't be found in the splendor of offerings but in a life rich with justice, mercy, and humility.

These elements—justice, kindness, and a relationship with God are tangible actions. Justice (mispat) calls us to be agents of fairness, advocates for the oppressed, and architects of right relationships. Kindness (hesed) invites us to love genuinely and loyally, reflecting the divine covenant in all our relationships. Walking humbly (halak) is a journey done with integrity, placing the divine will above our own.

These are dynamic acts. They call us to embody justice, to love with deep fidelity, and to walk with a humility that elevates our spirit. They challenge us to transform our lives and communities, reflecting the divine light in every act and interaction.

As we reflect on Micah's message, we can find new ways to incorporate a message of justice, kindness, and humility in our preaching and teaching. When we embrace these actions, we don't just fulfill ancient texts; we breathe life into them, crafting a world that mirrors the divine vision of harmony and peace.

We can do justice, love kindness, and walk humbly in the truth. It is how we discover the profound peace of living faithful to our calling.

The Meditation

Take a moment to find a quiet space to sit comfortably, free from distractions. Close your eyes gently. Begin by taking a deep, slow inhale, filling your lungs, and then exhale, releasing all the air and tension from your body. Do this breathing three times, focusing solely on your breath—feel the rise and fall of your chest, the air moving through your nostrils.

Now as you settle into a rhythm of calm breathing—inhale slowly, exhale slowly—reflect on the journey of the people of Israel as told by the prophet Micah, from bondage to freedom, from despair to hope. With each inhale, imagine drawing in hope and freedom; with each exhale, release any feelings of hopelessness or bondage that weigh on your spirit.

Consider the covenant with the divine, a pact filled with expectations of justice, mercy, and humility. Breathe in deeply, inhaling justice and compassion into your being. As you exhale, let go of any injustices or harshness you've held onto. Inhale, drawing in the humility to walk closely with the divine, and exhale any pride or ego.

As you breathe deeply, ponder Micah's call to embody these virtues daily. Think about how you can act justly, love mercy, and walk humbly in your interactions and decisions. Let each breath reinforce your commitment to these values, filling you with purpose and alignment with the divine will.

When you are ready, gently open your eyes, carrying the peace and resolve from this meditation into your day.

The Questions

1. How can you embody the principles of justice, mercy, and humility in your interactions with others this week?
2. How might integrating the values of justice, mercy, and humility into your daily routine impact your relationships and overall well-being?
3. How can deep, mindful breathing help you better align with the Spirit during stressful moments?

Chapter 15

Something New

Isaiah 43:16-19

In the heart of scripture, Isaiah warns the people of Israel about their preoccupation with past achievements. Indeed, they had experienced dramatic rescues and victories. From their exodus out of Egypt to the establishment under kings like David and Solomon, they had seen the hand of divine guidance shaping them into a nation tasked with exemplifying mercy, love, and care. Even in their imperfections, they were reminded that they were chosen to lead by example.

Yet through Isaiah, God urges a forward-looking vision: "Do not remember the former things or consider the things of old." This call resonates with clarity and purpose, for dwelling too much on what has been clouds our perception of what could be. In essence, being tethered to the past can stifle the birth of new possibilities.

This message is not just historical; it is profoundly relevant to us today. At a time when humanity grapples with issues ranging from environmental crises to social injustices, there is a divine impetus at work urging us to innovate and reform. Here are ways we see this transformative energy in action:

New technologies are being harnessed to address climate change and promote sustainable living, reminding us that our planet requires gratitude and care.

Movements for social justice are reshaping conversations, making us confront our collective failures in treating each other with dignity and respect.

Community-led initiatives like neighborhood gardens are tackling food scarcity issues, turning neglected spaces into areas of growth and sustenance. A new wave of entrepreneurship teaches young people the importance of financial wisdom and self-sufficiency.

The difficult conversations about racial history are becoming more prevalent, signaling a shift toward a more honest and inclusive narrative.

People are leveraging their resources and abilities to effect change everywhere, embodying the spirit of progress.

Isaiah's reminder is a timeless echo in our lives encouraging us to let go of the past to witness the unfolding of new wonders. No matter the challenges, we are urged not to lose heart. The journey forward is moving away from past errors and toward future opportunities. God's creativity is limitless; each day is a canvas for something new.

If history tells of miracles like paths made in wildernesses and seas parted to provide passage to new beginnings, then today is no less ripe for miracles. God's readiness to lead us through trials, to inspire new solutions, and to transcend old barriers is as present now as it was in the days of Isaiah.

We do not anchor ourselves to what has been; instead, we sail forward on the winds of divine inspiration. If you reach beyond your grasp of what you have imagined was unreachable, you will find yourself achieving more than you imagined. The call to forget the old is not just about leaving behind what no longer serves us but is about embracing the potential that each new day holds.

Each moment is ripe with potential; every day is a fresh opportunity for renewal and wonder. God's faithfulness and mercy are our daily bread, nourishing us to embrace the new work being done in us, for us, and through us.

Let this be a day to discover something new.

The Meditation

Begin with finding a comfortable place to sit or stand where you can feel grounded and present. Close your eyes gently, and turn your attention inward with a deep, cleansing breath. Inhale slowly through your nose, feeling your lungs expand with fresh possibilities. Exhale through your mouth, releasing the burdens of past achievements and the weight of old stories.

As you inhale, feel a sense of peace and renewal. As you breathe out, imagine letting go of what no longer serves you—past errors, outdated victories, and worn-out narratives. Inhale the courage to face new challenges; exhale the fear of unknown paths.

Continue to breathe deeply and feel more present with each breath. Let these words echo softly: "Do not remember the former things or consider the things of old." Let this be a call to embrace the now, open to the endless possibilities that await.

With each inhale, invite clarity and inspiration. With each exhale, release hesitation and doubt. Today, center yourself in boundless creativity. As you reach the end of this meditation, take one more deep breath, fully absorbing the spirit of progress and renewal.

When you are ready, gently open your eyes. Carry forward the strength and peace from this practice into all your actions and interactions.

The Questions
1. What past achievements are you holding onto that might be preventing you from embracing new opportunities?
2. How can you cultivate a mindset open to innovation and change in the face of current challenges?
3. What are the first steps you can take to actively move toward new possibilities that this day offers?

Chapter 16

Get in the Race

Philippians 3:12-14

On the journey of life, everyone has a unique path marked by destiny. This path is our calling, imbuing each moment with purpose, regardless of the hurdles we encounter. True to the human experience, these hurdles come in many forms, each a test of our resolve and dedication to our purpose.

Imagine life as a vast stadium filled with different kinds of people. Some are mere spectators, content to live vicariously through the achievements and lives of others. They find safety in the stands, far removed from the sweat and soil of the track, where the real action happens. They cheer and dream, but the race is not theirs to run.

Others stand aloof from the race, critiquing and making excuses. They point out the imperfections in the track or lament the lack of guidance, never stepping forward to take their mark. Fear of failure and a penchant for criticism keep them from experiencing the raw thrill of competition.

Then there are the solitary runners, who believe they can conquer the track alone. They acknowledge no coach or crowd, claiming every victory solely their own. Yet, this isolation can shadow even the brightest triumphs, for shared joy is diminished.

Among the runners, some seasoned veterans understand the enduring nature of the race. Their pace might have slowed, but their spirit remains undeterred. They run, seasoned by both victories and losses, offering slivers of wisdom to those willing to listen. Yet there are also the determined few who genuinely embrace the race. They acknowledge their imperfections, the less-than-ideal conditions, and the daunting obstacles ahead. They run not because the path is easy but because they refuse to be bystanders in their own lives. They run with hearts full of hope, propelled by a will that refuses to dim, even in the darkest times.

Paul the Apostle saw life similarly—a race marked by service and faith.

Despite lacking physical prowess, Paul was driven by a profound desire to serve, embracing his flaws as catalysts for growth. He viewed his life as a continuous race, a steadfast pursuit of Christ's love and service. Paul's mission was not about earthly acclaim but about striving toward divine grace and the betterment of his community. From Paul's journey, we draw invaluable lessons: the importance of goals rooted in service and spirituality, the acceptance of our human imperfections, and the commitment to press on despite them. Paul teaches us that our true strength lies in our resilience and our ability to stay focused on the spiritual prize ahead.

As leaders, we are called to press on with purpose. Our race is not just for ourselves but for all those we can touch with our ministry. It is a race of healing, mentoring, building, and transforming—not just lives but entire communities. In this grand race, we are participants, not spectators. Let us run with endurance the race set before us, inspired by those who have run before, like Paul, and most importantly, by Christ, who exemplified humility and service from his baptism to his ascension. This race is our mission, filled with endless possibilities to serve, love, and bring about change.

So lace up your shoes, step up to the starting line, and run with all the enthusiasm and dedication you can muster. The race is long, with many hurdles, but the reward is beyond measure. Let's run this race together, with eyes fixed on the prize, hearts open to love, and hands ready to serve.

The Meditation

Sit comfortably, finding a quiet space where you can be uninterrupted. Close your eyes gently. Begin to focus on your breath, taking a slow, deep inhale, allowing your chest and belly to expand. Then exhale slowly through your mouth, releasing any tension you might feel. With each breath, envision yourself at the starting line of a vast, open stadium. It is not just any race; it is the journey of your leadership.

As you inhale, draw in confidence and strength. As you exhale, let go of doubts and fears.

Imagine around you a crowd of spectators, some distant, observing from the safety of the stands. They choose not to engage directly with the challenges of the track. Acknowledge them, and then bring your focus back to your breath. Inhale deeply and see yourself choosing to step onto the track, ready to run. With every exhale, release criticism and fear of failure, letting these feelings dissolve into the air. You are here to participate fully, embracing each step of the path with resilience and hope.

As you breathe in again, think of the seasoned runners who have faced many races, their pace seasoned by victories and losses. Draw strength from their wisdom, letting it fuel your spirit as you prepare to move forward. With each breath, reaffirm your commitment to not just run but to run with purpose. It is a race of healing, mentoring, and building—a transformation for yourself and the community you serve.

Continue to breathe deeply, maintaining this focus. With each inhale, gather strength and hope. With each exhale, release anything that holds you back.

When you are ready, slowly bring your awareness back to the present. Open your eyes, feeling refreshed and renewed, prepared to step forward with purpose and passion in your leadership journey.

The Questions
1. What challenges or fears have you faced recently in your role, and how can embracing vulnerability transform these experiences into opportunities for growth?
2. How can you deepen your impact within your community by embodying the qualities of resilience and determination?
3. Reflect on a recent situation where you felt like a spectator rather than a participant. What steps can you take to become more actively engaged in your personal and professional life?

Chapter 17

Another Perspective

John 1:1-14

According to John, the gospel's narrative diverges significantly from the accounts of Matthew and Luke. No angels are heralding the birth of Jesus, no shepherds witnessing the event, nor any wise men following a star to a humble manger. This absence of a picturesque nativity scene might seem lacking to some, yet John's focus is profoundly directed elsewhere. He centers on the profound implications of what the birth of Jesus signifies for humanity.

John's message is clear and potent in John 1:12: "But to all who received him, who believed in his name, he gave power to become children of God" (NRSV).

This declaration isn't about bloodlines or human will but a divine transformation available through faith. John isn't as concerned with the physical circumstances of Jesus's birth as he is with the rebirth of every believer into the family of God.

What does it mean, then, to become a child of God? It means to embrace the characteristics of the divine, reflecting the nature of the Creator in our actions and being. We become manifestations of love, peace, truth, and justice because these qualities define God's essence.

Embodying these traits, we affirm our role as active participants in creation.

As children of God, our identity is not shackled by our past mistakes, societal labels, or the destructive behavior of others. Instead, we are defined by our relationship with God, rooted in Jesus's transformative teachings. Embracing these teachings, we see beyond our immediate circumstances to our eternal identity in light and love.

This identity empowers us to act in love despite hatred, find peace amid chaos, and bring joy in the face of sorrow. It calls us to create beauty where there is ugliness, to speak kindness instead of criticism, and to foster unity over division. It is a call to live courageously, regardless of fear, embodying the light of Christ in every aspect of our lives.

We are mindful to transcend the trivial and the transient to live out the profound truth of our divine inheritance. As the old hymn "Jesus, the Light of the World" suggests, we walk in the light, basking in the "beautiful light" where "the dewdrops of mercy shine bright," and let us shine this light by day and night, embodying Jesus, the true light of the world.

Today, as inheritors of God's profound blessings, let us live fully as children of God, letting our light shine forth in every moment and every place.

The Meditation

Pause for a moment. Take a deep breath in, and as you exhale slowly, consider the unique perspective of John's gospel. Unlike the traditional narratives, there are no angels, shepherds, or wise men. Instead, the focus shifts profoundly to what the birth of Jesus truly means for humanity. Inhale deeply and reflect on John's powerful message: "But to all who received him, who believed in his name, he gave the power to become children of the divine." This transformation, offered to everyone through faith, surpasses ordinary human distinctions and origins.

Breathe in peace and exhale any tension. Breathe out love, peace, truth, and justice. These are the ideals of your nature, reflecting the sacred in every action and decision. As you breathe slowly, let go of past errors and societal labels. Your identity is rooted not in these transient markers but in a transformative relationship, a profound understanding of your eternal worth.

With each inhale, embrace this truth. With each exhale, release what holds you back. You are called to manifest beauty in places of ugliness, to offer peace where there is chaos, and to extend joy amid sorrow. Feel the courage rising with each breath. You are equipped to live boldly and authentically, a true reflection of divine light, regardless of external circumstances.

Now breathe in deeply and hold that breath for a moment. Feel the potential within you to illuminate every corner of your world. As you exhale, commit to radiating this inner light wherever you go, making visible the invisible grace that guides you. Embrace this meditation as you step into each new day, remembering that you are a profound reflection of the divine, capable of shaping the world with every breath you take.

The Questions
1. What does it mean to embody traits like love, peace, truth, and justice in daily interactions, and how can these qualities influence your personal and professional relationships?
2. Reflect on the moments when external circumstances or societal labels have challenged your identity. How can you reinforce a sense of independence despite external pressures?
3. Consider the concept of transformation through acceptance and belief. How can embracing new teachings or perspectives lead to profound personal growth and change?

Chapter 18

A Radical Kind of Love

Matthew 5:43-45

Our stories do not begin where we are today; they start in the heart of ancient civilizations. The narratives spun around our past, often simplified and sanitized, threaten to obscure the vast tapestry of experiences that define us.

Amid efforts to dilute our historical narratives in education, the responsibility to impart a new understanding of our past to the next generation becomes even more paramount. It's not just about recounting events; it's about reclaiming a narrative as ancient as time. Our children need to grasp the full spectrum of their heritage, which stretches far beyond the confines of adversity into the realms of kings and scholars.

Reflecting on this brings to mind the teachings of Jesus, who ministered primarily within his community, addressing the specific needs and injustices that plagued his people. His mission was clear in its focus yet radical in its reach, emphasizing a profound and proactive love. He spoke to a people familiar with oppression and fragmentation, encouraging unity that could only be forged through genuine and sometimes radical love.

In communities today, just as in Nazareth, divisions, strife, betrayals, and misunderstandings hinder collective progress. The societal pressures that pitted neighbors against each other under Roman rule find their echoes in modern systemic inequalities that disproportionately affect marginalized communities. Jesus's response was to teach a love that transcends the superficial and cuts to the core of human dignity. He urged his followers to see beyond immediate grievances and act compassionately and understanding, even toward those deemed enemies.

The Greek concept of *agape*—unconditional love—was revolutionary in its implications. It wasn't merely about tolerating one's enemies but actively seeking their well-being.

This kind of love challenges us to look at those within our circles, perhaps even within our reflections, who might oppose us yet are integral to our shared story.

In this spirit, the call to love radically within our communities reflects faith and a blueprint for action. We are urged to move beyond the barriers of distrust and division to forge alliances where there might have been animosity. The teachings of Jesus call for resistance to evil and to advocate for an active proliferation of good.

To love our communities radically is to commit ourselves to the welfare of all its members, to seek justice where there is inequity, to offer healing where there is hurt, and to provide enlightenment where there is ignorance. It means stepping into the fray, not as bystanders but as bearers of light, armed with a profound love for our people and heritage.

Thus as we reflect on the challenges that face us as a society and as individuals within it, let us remember the strength that can be harnessed through a community united by love. Let us not forget that in every moment of injustice, there is an opportunity for advocacy; in every moment of misunderstanding, a chance for clarity; and in every moment of division, a call for reconciliation.

In the ongoing struggle for justice and equity, let this radical love be our guiding principle as we strive to embody the virtues Jesus exemplified. This is how we honor our past, navigate our present, and forge a future that is inclusive, respectful, and imbued with an understanding of love.

The Meditation

Take a deep breath and allow yourself to be present in this moment. Inhale slowly, feeling the air fill your lungs, and as you exhale, consider the depth of your heritage, stretching back to ancient civilizations, rich with the narratives of kings and scholars. These stories are relics and the underpinnings of who you are today.

Inhale, remembering your responsibility to pass on this profound understanding to the next generation with each breath. Exhale slowly, releasing any tension, and reflect on how this knowledge shapes the community you serve.

Inhale deeply, drawing in the strength from these ancient roots. As you hold that breath, think of Jesus, who taught love and unity within his community amid oppression and division. Let this breath out slowly, contemplating the radical love he advocated—love that seeks to coexist and actively uplift and heal.

Now breathe in once more, embracing the challenges and divisions within your community. Exhale, pondering how you can embody this same radical love. It's about seeing past immediate grievances, offering compassion, and understanding even toward those you find difficult.

As you continue to breathe deeply, consider the concept of agape—unconditional, proactive love. With each inhale, see yourself extending love to your community. With each exhale, imagine breaking down the barriers of distrust and division, building alliances, and fostering understanding.

As you inhale, realize your potential to step into your role and purpose, not just as a bystander but as a bearer of light and love. Hold this breath, feeling its weight and warmth. As you let it go, envision yourself advocating for justice, healing wounds, and enlightening those around you.

Each breath is a moment to reflect on how this radical love transforms your community and yourself. It's a call to live out the virtues that unite people, mend divisions, and forge a future marked by respect and profound unity.

With your final breath in this meditation, gather all the love and strength from your reflections. As you exhale, commit to carrying this love forward, honoring your past, navigating the present, and shaping a future where everyone is recognized, respected, and cherished. This mindful practice of radical love is your path to transforming your community.

The Questions
1. How can radical love be applied in your daily interactions to actively uplift and unite your community?
2. What historical narratives of your heritage can empower and inspire your community today? How might you incorporate these stories into your leadership and teaching?
3. Reflecting on the divisions within your community, what practical steps can you take to foster reconciliation and build alliances among those who might initially oppose each other?

Chapter 19

Beginnings

Matthew 3:13-17

In the rhythms of life, we often encounter the necessity to start afresh, just as Jesus did at pivotal moments of his journey. Starting anew—whether it's a new job, school, church, or perhaps a completely new environment—brings a mix of anticipation and trepidation. This combination of excitement and fear is not unfamiliar in human experience. It echoes the trepidation of the Hebrews at the brink of the Red Sea, contemplating the daunting unknown yet propelled by the promise of liberation.

The essence of human nature—our mental, emotional, and psychological makeup—can make us resist change. It's a defensive mechanism, perhaps designed to protect us from the unpredictable. Yet embracing new beginnings requires courage, preparation, strength, and resolve. In the Gospel of Mark, we observe Jesus at such a commencement: his baptism. This event isn't merely a ritual; it marks the beginning of his profound engagement with humanity—a mission filled with healing, liberation, and the relentless pursuit of justice.

Seeking divine approval may not involve hearing an actual voice but sensing an inner affirmation from God. We turn away from personal desires and societal illusions toward a focus on service and spiritual fulfillment. Jesus's baptism by John was not just an individual act of repentance but a public declaration of his dedication to God's path and serving others.

As Jesus prepared for his mission, he embraced humility and servitude, necessary not only for his time but equally vital for us today. This preparation wasn't devoid of challenges. Like Jesus, who was tested in the wilderness, our commitments are often tested. We are challenged to prove our dedication through trials, demonstrating that materialism, ego, and power do not sway us.

This narrative isn't just historical; it's instructional. It beckons us to reflect on our paths and the preparations we must undertake.

Embracing a new phase in life or ministry involves several critical steps that echo the movements Jesus exemplified. Acting with humility requires a decisive break from past fears and embracing new possibilities. It's about letting go of doubts and welcoming a life filled with creative joy and service, acknowledging that our true calling is to transcend the mundane pursuits of the world.

Authentic leadership follows the inner light, fueled by passion and dedication to God's will. This means moving beyond our desires to serve the greater good, impacting lives through genuine acts of kindness and compassion without expecting anything in return.

We feel empowered to fulfill our potential, dreaming boldly and pursuing those dreams with the conviction that our actions are meaningful and aligned with God's vision. We align closer with God's purposes, and there is a sense in which we feel affirmed to lead and inspire others.

The Meditation

Take a moment to breathe deeply. Inhale slowly, recognizing the fresh start before you, just as pivotal moments marked new beginnings in ancient stories. Exhale any hesitation, embracing the excitement and concern accompanying each new chapter—a new job, community, or role.

Inhale again and consider your nature, how it sometimes holds you back from embracing change because of fear of the unknown. Exhale, release the fear and summon the courage and strength required for what lies ahead. Remember, every meaningful start is a commitment to a higher purpose.

As you prepare to step into your new role, breathe deeply, filling yourself with the resolve to meet the challenges of any great endeavor. Exhale doubts and embrace humility and service, essential qualities for any leader. Inhale, drawing in the strength to forego personal desires and societal illusions for a focus on service and spiritual fulfillment.

Now as you reflect on your journey, recognize each step is a test of your dedication. With every breath out, let go of materialism, ego, and the lure of power. Breathe in the fortitude to overcome these trials.

Embrace a moment of quiet and stillness. Breathe in, acknowledging your readiness to rise above mundane pursuits and touch lives through genuine acts of service. Exhale, and with it, release any need for recognition, embracing servant leadership.

Finally, breathe deeply and trust the silent affirmation of your calling. Each step forward from a place of humility and service aligns you with your highest potential.

Take one more deep breath. Feel empowered as you step into your role, ready to inspire and lead, recognizing that each new beginning is an opportunity to manifest your commitment to a life of service and leadership. With each exhale, feel renewed and ready to embrace the journey ahead.

The Questions

1. What personal desires or societal expectations might you need to release to fully embrace your new role or venture?
2. How can you demonstrate humility and servant leadership in your daily interactions to foster a positive environment for yourself and those around you?
3. Reflecting on past challenges, what lessons have you learned

that can be applied to your current or upcoming transition to ensure it is successful and fulfilling?

Chapter 20

Passing the Peace

John 20:19-23

As dusk fell and the streets emptied of Jesus's disciples, these followers, who had placed their trust in Jesus, found themselves leaderless. The hope of liberation from Roman tyranny and relief from the strictures of Jewish law was no longer among them. The teacher who had enlightened them about love had disappeared. Their desire for the restoration of Israel had been extinguished. Jesus was gone, and with him, their courage and clarity.

In the solitude of hiding, the disciples became fugitives, recognized and sought after for their close ties to Jesus. They had dared to proclaim him the true king of the Jews, a declaration tantamount to sedition. As did the Roman authorities, the religious leaders who opposed Jesus now pursued his followers. The disciples, overwhelmed by the magnitude of their crisis, sought refuge in the shadows, disappearing into a world that had rejected their message of compassion, forgiveness, and love. They secluded themselves in a locked room, shrouded in guilt and fear. They had abandoned Jesus in his hour of greatest need, retreating into silence even as he stood alone before his accusers. Peter, who had once boldly stepped onto the water at Jesus's beckoning, quickly succumbed to doubt and fear. And Judas, whose betrayal was driven by political intrigue and greed, had forsaken the spiritual journey.

Confronting our limitations in times of crisis is a profound, though painful, human experience. We are capable of withstanding any challenge. Yet when faced with immediate threats, our survival instincts prevail, and our cherished principles may be swiftly discarded. It was the disciples' plight—they failed their teacher, ideals, and themselves. They faced the stark reality of their shortcomings in that locked room, surrounded by fear and uncertainty.

However, the narrative shifts when Jesus enters this room of despair. His greeting, "Peace be with you," carries the weight of tradition and deep spiritual significance. This peace—eirēnē in Greek, shalom in Hebrew—is not merely an absence of conflict but a profound state of holistic well-being. Jesus offered this peace to his disciples, an invitation to calm their troubled minds and find solace in unity and purpose.

Jesus spoke to them of a life beyond fear and self-reproach. "As the Father has sent me, so I send you," he declared, urging them to transcend their anxieties and embrace a higher calling. He reminded them that the fears and scenarios conjured by their anxious minds were distortions of reality, shadows that obscured the light of truth.

When Jesus breathed on them, the breath of God—ruah in Hebrew, a life-giving force that animated creation itself—was a moment of profound empowerment. This breath, or emphysao in Greek, was not just a transfer of air but a transformative spiritual wind, gentle yet powerful, stirring their souls and rekindling their purpose.

In contemporary times, the church, too, seems to retreat into shadows, influenced by fear and fragmented by divisive politics. At times, it has strayed from Christ's foundational teachings—teachings centered on love, justice, and compassion. Yet the invitation to peace and empowerment that Jesus extended to his disciples still extends to us. The Holy Spirit continues to flow through every fiber of the church, calling us to reclaim and live out the radical message of Christ.

We are invited to reflect deeply on this divine presence and power within us. The Holy Spirit is ready to stir within us a renewal of faith and action:

> Come, Holy Spirit, fill us with your power.
> Come, Holy Spirit, grace us with your presence.
> Come, Holy Spirit, inspire us to stand for righteousness.
> Come, Holy Spirit, reinvigorate our zeal for justice and love.

In this reflection today, we seek ways to restore peace and to live out our mission in a world that yearns for the healing touch of divine love.

The Meditation

As you comfortably sit quietly, imagine yourself among those early disciples of women and men, feeling alone and uncertain without your leader. The teacher who guided you on the path of love is no longer present, and the promise of a renewed homeland seems lost. In this moment, you find yourself a fugitive, hiding from those who misunderstand your message of love and compassion.

Inhale deeply, recognizing the weight of fear and doubt that has settled upon your shoulders. Exhale slowly, letting go of the guilt and despair that cloud your thoughts. You are in a locked room, your heart pounding with uncertainty. Breathe in again, feeling the coolness of the air, and with each exhale, release the tension that has built up within.

Now picture a figure of peace entering this room of shadows—offering words of comfort: "Peace be with you." This peace is the absence of conflict and a deep, encompassing calm that settles over your spirit. Inhale this peace, letting it fill you with purpose and unity.

Exhale your doubts. Your challenges and fears are not the full extent of your reality. They are mere shadows, and with each breath, you can push them further into the periphery of your awareness.

When the figure breathes upon you, feel the warmth of that breath like a gentle, revitalizing wind. It is not merely air but a force of life, empowering you from within. With each breath in, draw in strength and clarity. With each breath out, expel hesitation and fear.

In the stillness that follows, know that you are not alone. The spirit of peace and empowerment fills you, urging you to rise beyond the crises of the moment. Inhale courage; exhale timidity. You are called to live out a message of love and justice, to stand firm in the face of adversity.

As you continue to breathe deeply, feel renewed and ready to carry forth the message of peace into a world that desperately needs it. Let each breath remind you of your purpose and the peace that guides and sustains you through every challenge.

The Questions

1. What fears or challenges currently feel overwhelming in your life, and how can you address them with the same calm and peace that was sought in times of distress?
2. Reflect on when you felt alone or misunderstood in your convictions. How did you navigate that experience, and what strengths did you discover about yourself during that time?
3. Consider the concept of peace as more than just the absence of conflict. What does true peace look like in your daily interactions, and how can you actively cultivate it within your community?

Chapter 21

Do Not Forget to Remember

2 Peter 1:12

We return to where we began. In the heart of sacred reflection lies a profound recognition of our lineage—of those who have endured and transcended the brutal realities of life with a resilience that has birthed unparalleled wisdom and artistry. Our ancestors were not just survivors; they were creators of change, dynamic leaders, innovators, and healers who understood the earth's gifts long before modern medicine reached them.

Honoring our ancestors means recognizing their presence in our daily lives, just as our ancient ancestors remembered theirs. Our memories and the kind words we've heard about those who sought to live righteous lives are part of an active engagement with their stories—stories that hold lessons of strength and foresight. They carry stories of joy and pain, success and failure—each a guidepost for navigating our lives and informing our decisions. They have bequeathed to us life stories of inherited diseases and adverse conditions, showing us that honoring them involves more than remembrance. We must implement echoes of their wisdom and fortitude.

Moreover, our ancestors provide a roadmap for personal and collective healing. They teach us to release regrets, learn from every experience, and embrace our strengths and vulnerabilities. Their lives remind us that while existence can be harsh, we have inherited the strength to overcome adversity. Through their example, we can face our challenges and transform our lives.

In the solitude of prayer or the quiet moments of reflection, engage in conversations with those who came before you. Thank them for their sacrifices, their courage, and their wisdom. Acknowledge even those ancestors whose lives were marked by difficulty and strife, for they, too, contribute to the rich legacy from which we draw strength.

When life is heavy with disappointments and hope seems a distant flicker, we should call their names. In doing so, we summon their enduring spirit and weave their enduring strength into our current trials.

So we speak their names in times of challenge and celebration alike. We remember them in times when we need courage. We call their names when we forget our purpose. We call their names to ignite the light of hope in our darkest moments.

Choosing to remember is to find peace in the power of their stories of hope and transformation.

The Meditation

As you settle into a moment of quiet reflection, allow yourself to breathe deeply. Inhale the resilience and wisdom that your ancestors carried through their trials. Exhale the burdens you have inherited, transforming them into lessons of strength and perseverance.

Feel the weight of history in your breath as you contemplate and remember those ancestors who live in your bones, your DNA. Inhale again, drawing in the legacy of leadership, innovation, and healing that your forebears crafted, understanding nature's remedies long before the world acknowledged them. Exhale any hesitation to embrace this vast lineage stretching across continents and centuries, admitting that these roots are not lost, merely waiting to be reclaimed.

As you continue to breathe, reflect on the journeys of those like Moses and Abraham, who walked paths of liberation and promise.

Let each inhale draw in their courage and conviction, and with each exhale, release the fears that bind you to the past.

Breathe in the stories of joy, pain, success, and failure that your ancestors lived. Allow these stories to fill you with the knowledge to navigate your own life, teaching you to prevent what can be avoided and to replicate what brought them success. As you breathe out, let go of past regrets, embracing the lessons learned from each experience.

Now pause to thank those who came before you. With each breath, honor their struggles and their triumphs. Remember their faces, their voices, and the life lessons they imparted that still resonate within you.

And when you feel overwhelmed by the challenges of your journey, whisper their names. Call upon their strength and wisdom to renew your spirit. Let their names be your anchor, reconnecting you to a lineage of survival and resilience.

As you open your eyes and return from this meditation, carry the power of their stories, allowing them to inspire and guide you as you write your narrative of hope and transformation. Remember, in the quiet stillness of your breath lies the connection to countless generations whose endurance and spirit empower you today.

The Questions

1. How can you actively incorporate the wisdom and resilience of your ancestors into your daily decision-making and leadership?
2. In what ways have you acknowledged or perhaps neglected your community's rich cultural heritage and historical roots? What steps can you take to deepen your connection and understanding?
3. Reflect on the struggles and triumphs of your ancestors. How do their stories influence your perspective on the challenges and opportunities you face today?

Remember to take a moment to breathe.

About the Authors

Rev. Daniel T. Hembree, PhD

As a contemplative pastor, leader, and professor of pastoral care and counseling, Dr. Daniel T. Hembree has served in the church and academic setting for more than thirty years. Dr. Hembree serves as dean and assistant professor of pastoral care, counseling, and theology at Dickerson-Green Theological Seminary. Before he was appointed dean, Dr. Hembree was the program administrator for the Environmental Justice Institute at Allen University. He is also the pastor of the historic John Wesley United Methodist Church in Greenville, South Carolina.

Dr. Hembree began his academic career at Claflin University. He served as the director of the Center for the Theological Exploration of Vocation, chair of the Philosophy and Religion Department, and chaplain of the James and Dorothy Z. Elmore Chapel. He has also served as both dean and faculty member of the Youth Theological Initiative of the Candler School of Theology at Emory University; interim director of the Center for the Church and the Black Experience; adjunct instructor in pastoral care and counseling at Garrett-

Evangelical Theological Seminary; adjunct lecturer in religion at Northwestern University; visiting professor in religion at the University of South Carolina; and chair of the Graduate Program in Urban Ministries at Martin University.

Dr. Hembree holds a Bachelor of Arts in biological anthropology from the University of Michigan; a Master of Divinity from Garrett-Evangelical Theological Seminary; a graduate certificate in African Studies; and a Doctor of Philosophy in religion, society, and personality from Northwestern University. He is a member of the American Academy of Religion, the Society for the Study of Black Religion, and the Society of Pastoral Theology.

He is married to Dr. Amenti Sujai, associate professor of church history at Dickerson-Green Theological Seminary and the pastor of the Greer Circuit in Greer, South Carolina. The have a blended family of five children and six grandchildren.

Rev. Amenti Sujai, PhD

Hailing from the vibrant city of Chicago, Illinois, Dr. Amenti Sujai embarked on her academic journey at Southern Illinois University earning a Bachelor of Arts in psychology. Following her undergraduate accomplishments, she enrolled in Garrett-Evangelical Theological Seminary, culminating in the attainment of a Master of Theological Studies.

Further advancing her scholarly pursuits, Dr. Sujai was conferred a Doctor of Philosophy from Northwestern University. Her specialized academic focus within the field of religious and theological studies led her to concentrate on areas such as religious history and ethics.

Currently, Dr. Sujai holds the valued position of associate professor of church history at Dickerson-Green Theological Seminary.

Prior to joining the faculty at Allen University, she had a notable tenure as an associate professor in the Department of Philosophy and Religion. She served as the associate director of the Center for Vocational Reflection at Claflin University, located in Orangeburg, South Carolina.

In addition to her academic roles, Dr. Sujai fulfills her pastoral calling as a commissioned elder and current shepherd of Greer Circuit in Greer, South Carolina. She has also extended her ministry to offer specialized workshops on guided meditation and mindfulness.

Dr. Sujai is married to Rev. Daniel Troy Hembree, PhD, a distinguished clergyman from Detroit, Michigan. Dr. Hembree serves as the pastor of John Wesley United Methodist Church in Greenville, South Carolina. Their family is a harmonious blend, comprising four sons and one daughter, further blessed with six grandchildren. The extended family resides in both Chicago, Illinois, and Atlanta, Georgia.

www.ingramcontent.com/pod-product-compliance
Lightning Source LLC
Chambersburg PA
CBHW070207100426
42743CB00013B/3082